How to file for VA Disability Claims

Filing A Claim with the VA - What To Do

If you do the following you will have a better than average chance of winning your claim.

1.   Gather All Military, Private and VA Medical Records

Gather all the military, private and VA medical records (get copies made). Make a Privacy Act Request at your VA Regional Office. They will have a copy of your Military Medical Record. Request Copies of Military Personnel Records http://www.archives.gov/research_room/vetrecs/ to include all restricted records, counseling statements and evaluation reports. Do not expect the VA to automatically have your medical records from your active duty. Those records will need to be requested either from your unit of assignment or the staging facility in St Louis, MO by completing an SF180. Call or visit your Service Officer from DAV, VFW, or American Legion for this form. Mail the SF 180 to the appropriate address listed on the back of the Form.

http://contacts.gsa.gov/webforms.nsf/0/6A748D94A429DE1085256CB10043FB7B/$file/sf180_f .pdf

Written letters may be mailed to: The National Personnel Records Center (Military Personnel Records) 9700 Page Avenue St. Louis, MO 63132-5100. Response time varies dependent upon the complexity of your request, the availability of records, and workload. Please do not send a follow-up request before 90 days have elapsed as it may cause further delays. http://www.archives.gov/research_room/vetrecs/index.html

2.   Obtaining medical records that are already within the VA system

Obtaining medical records that are already within the VA system can be achieved by faxing or mailing a written request providing a "release of information" to the VA Records Section. State the dates of records you're looking for, doctors' reports, lab and X-ray reports; your name, address, phone number, social security number, and signature. Label your request as a Privacy Act Request.

3.   Go to your civilian doctor

Go to your civilian doctor; have him/her perform a C&P exam. Download a copy of the exam from the VA web site http://www.vba.va.gov/bln/21/Benefits/exams/index.htm. Have your doctor perform the entire test you should have. The VA rarely does the necessary tests. You need to have this done because the VA will not do a complete C&P examination. See #4 for further explanation

4. Get statements from all private doctors or other medical provider

Get statements from all private doctors or other medical provider, have them state that your problems and how they could be service connected. Get more than one doctor to say the same thing then write if two doctors say the same thing, then the reasonable doubt (§3.102) rule should apply and you state the probability is slim that the issue ISN'T service connected. Doctors don't like to be pushed to give tenuous opinions - unless they are lousy doctors who will swear to anything. And the bottom line is that the opinion won't be worth spit unless he has medical findings to support it. It is awfully easy to disregard a "definite" opinion given by some yo-yo who hasn't made a decent exam nor recited any findings to give that opinion a sound basis. You need to tell the doctor what you were exposed to in the military. If you have documentation, then show that to the doctor, then ask the doctor to assume you were exposed to this hazard in service, and this is his work and personal history where he did not have other similar exposures, then assuming those things to be true ask the doctor to express his opinion based on reasonable medical certainty as to the cause of his condition? If the doctor is uncertain, then you need to him/she to say he/she it is probable. Obviously the more evidence the better. The fact is that one opinion of probable, based on the right assumptions and medical facts and findings, is enough to carry the proof because probable means that it is more likely than not, and the legal system operates on belief that truth is that which is most likely. Medical facts means the doctor can't say it's a particular disease without the required blood tests, cat/MRI scans, and whatever is necessary to prove the doctors opinion.

An example would be, if the doctor says you have cancer and when there has been no cat scan, no biopsy, no blood test of antigen - looking pale, or an undocumented complaint doesn't cut it. Or, to state it differently, when there are complaints that are not documented by physical findings, the doc can talk all day about how disabled this man is (because he says he is), and that really is unpersuasive.

To get VA compensation benefits for service connected disability, there is a three part test.
First, you must have a disability at the present time that has been diagnosed medically.
Second, there must have been a disease, injury or event in the service.
Third, there must be a nexus. This means that the current medical condition is related to the in service medical condition. This may include disabilities that are secondary conditions, due to a disability that is service connected.

There are exceptions. Connective tissue diseases exist which cannot be documented. There a doctor can say in his/her letter to the adjudicator: "the complaints are persistent, and this person who used to be happy and outgoing and very active has now adopted a very restricted lifestyle. There is a recognized medical condition called xxx. It causes the kinds of things which force a person into that sort of lifestyle." There is no known test to identify and diagnose this illness (the doctor needs to be direct the comments to either a Judge or adjudicator by talking in the first person) The doctor should state he "believes in this person" and he/she should state "If you also believe her complaints and that she now lives this lifestyle, then you have to believe she has this disabling condition."

5.   Get statements from anyone

Get statements from anyone who knows you and your issues. Write your own statement too! Have these individuals state how the problems affect you (example: It is hard to bend over, or squat, or hear, etc.). This includes your wife, kids, parents, co-workers even the guy/gal walking along the street. All of these people can contribute! All their statements are evidence that must be considered. If you have them put their phone number down on the statement and request the adjudicator to call (not if they have any questions), the adjudicator is required to call. If they don't call, you have grounds for appeal. The medical facts and findings speak louder than any of this testimony, and the veterans own testimony is quite powerful in describing the effect of this proven medical condition. The VA doctor's report that seeks to negate the claim is wide open to attack when he fails to do procedures or make determinative tests.

6.   Get the Vet Center Records

If you have been going to a Vet Center, get their records. They are independent of the VA medical system (CAPRI) so you need to get a statement or copy of your provider's notes or both from your treating Social Worker.

7.   Vocational Rehabilitation

If you have gone to Vocational Rehabilitation (Voc Rehab), you were evaluated by them too. Do a Privacy Act request and get all copies of evaluations and anything else (to include reports of contact [ROC]). The Voc Rehab evaluations carry some weight, since they are independent evaluations. Get copies of the contractor evaluations (the people that did the Voc Rehab screening) and the VA's Voc Rehab evaluations.

8.   Legal Research

Go to http://www.findlaw.com or http://www.veteransresources.net/database.html or http://www.va.gov/vbs.bva/ and look up all Board of Veteran Appeal, Court of Veteran Appeals, US District Court, US Court of Appeals and Supreme Court decisions that affect your issues. These legal opinions as well as the courts opinions narrows the focus of how the adjudicator can look at the evidence. Use these sites to support your other evidence. Do your own legal research! If you don't have access to the internet or are not internet savvy, you can get copies of any appeals and decisions from the VA. They can be requested from Veteran Benefits Office or the Adjudication Office. A simple phone call to one of those offices, explaining that you are requesting a copy of those records for your own file should be sufficient. Keep the information of who you talked with and their phone/fax numbers and addresses in your notebook for ready reference! Again, you may need to provide this request in writing, but this can usually be accomplished by phone or fax. Some Service Officers from DAV, VFW, or American Legion will do this for you, but don't depend entirely on them!   Some mental health records are kept separate from the main medical records, so again, you may need to call the Mental Health Clinic in your VA to request copies of those records from that office.

9.   Statements From VA Personnel

If you have been seeing a counselor at the VA Hospital, then get him/her to write you a statement of how bad they think you are. Plus, write up a statement on your own; let the adjudicator know about your background, your stressors and how this affects your daily life. Counselors are sometimes skeptical that people are acting out, pretending, not real. If the guy is really bogus, you might do better not to ask, but in truth, further questioning may well reveal that the skeptical counselor really believes the guy is pretty bad off or he wouldn't be going through all of this. That it is the stress of daily life that drives him to it. And NO counselor ever treats a death threat as anything other than real!

10.   SF 180

Use our system to create a customized order form to request information from your or your relative's, military personnel records. You may use this system if you are: A military veteran, or Next of kin of a deceased, former member of the military The next of kin can be any of the following: surviving spouse that has not remarried, father, mother, son, daughter, sister, or brother. If you are not the veteran or next of kin, you must complete the Standard Form 180 (SF 180). You can obtain this form from Fax-on-Demand, or download it, then mail or fax it to the appropriate address on the form.

The SF 180 may be photocopied as needed. Please submit a separate request (either SF 180 or letter) for each individual whose records are being requested. You may submit more than one request per envelope or fax. How to Initiate a Request for Military Personnel Records: Click on the "Request Military Records" button to start. This will launch a separate window. Enter the required information in the system to create your customized request form. There are 4 steps that you need to navigate. The system will guide you through the steps and tell you exactly which step you are on. Print, sign and date the signature verification area of your customized form. If you don't have a printer, have a pen and paper handy and we will guide you through the process. This is important because the Privacy Act of 1974 (5 U.S.C. 552a) requires that all requests for records and information be submitted in writing. Each request must be signed and dated by the veteran or next of kin. Mail or fax your signature verification forms to us, and we will process your request. You must do this within the first 20 days of entering your request, or your request will be removed from our system.

11.   Reviewing Your Military Records

Review your military medical records and make a list of every ailment that you had while on active duty. Note each biohazardous exposure you may have had. For example, If you used cosmoline on everything to protect it from rust, and then we would be in carbon tetrachloride up to the elbows because that was what used to clean it off. Carbon tet is cancer producing. I am sure there are many other examples.

12.   Cross Reference All your Military Ailments With Your Civilian Ailments

Cross reference all you military ailments with your civilian ailments. If the problem persists or a secondary issue has cropped up as a result of the issue that developed during your time in the military then you need to apply for that issue (as a secondary issue). An example of a secondary issue would be if you hurt your right knee and had to put weight on your left knee and now the knee is damaged. You can claim the left knee as a secondary issue to the injured right knee.

13.   Downloading

Go to the VA web site and down load all the Fast Letters, Memo's and any other documentation that will support your case. www.va.gov.

14.   Go to the DAV, PVA and any other VSO Web Site

Go to the DAV, PVA and any other VSO web sites and bookmark them (and down load anything related to your claims).

15.   WARMS

Go to http://www.warms.vba.va.gov/bookc.html Look up what your issue is and determine the percentage that you want to apply for. Now 98% of the Veteran Service Rep's (VSR's) will tell you not to give a percentage, but if you don't ask for a percentage and you are awarded 0% for an issue, you can't complain because they gave you exactly what you asked for. If the adjudicator denies your issue and you did not ask for a certain percentage, then you have to prove the VA didn't follow proper procedure (this is very hard to prove). Your VSR will tell you that the law can change. If it increases then just fax, email (w/receipt) or mail in an updated request. If the percentage decreases, you don't need to do anything. The Veterans Claims Assistance Act of 2000 allows the law that is most favorable to you to be applied to your claim so doesn't change your percentage.

16.   Current law favors the Vet.

The VA fights it but you can use this to your advantage. Invoke VCAA. Read, understand and learn what VCAA can do for you. If you are within a year of the VCAA letter you received, then you have rights to reopen old cases, don't let the time limit pass.

17.   You need to tell your story

You need to tell your story as to how you were injured. You need to compile all your evidence by issue. Yellow highlight those portions that pertains to you and your issues. Cite this in your narrative. You need to write up a narrative of how you were injured, under what circumstances (Who, What, When and How). List anyone who might have witnessed it. If you have a phone number or address, you need to provide that with your statement, cite the times you went to the medial facility, and later the follow-up care you have received from your private doctor. Invoke the reasonable doubt clause as well as all legal citations and regulations that support your claim VCAA. Site VBA and Court of Appeals legal cases that support your claim that you are entitled to a certain percentage rating. You will refer to evidence that you collected. Review the ratings percentages. Think of your worst day (pain, etc.) and rate yourself on that basis. After a few years your pain will probably be at that level, unless you can get the symptoms reversed somehow. Look up medical studies to support your claim and provide those studies to help in the adjudication process. VA or DoD or NIH medical studies are the best. It's hard to argue with yourself when yourself (the government) has come to the conclusion that the problem exists and what the symptoms are (which are the same symptoms you're reporting).

18.   Eligibility

You are entitled to claim all periods of active duty, all periods covered under Vocational Rehabilitation and any injuries suffered under the care of the VA for the purposes of disability claims (issues). You need to list all periods of active duty, to include ADT and reserve time. There are limited benefits for non-active duty personnel. By stating the periods of active duty, and providing documentation (such as copies of orders), you will increase your chances of winning your claim.

19.   C&P Examinations

 Go to the C&P office at your local VA Hospital (if you're too far away, having them either email or fax to you the exam criteria). Go to your private doctor. Have him do the C&P exam the correct way. Make sure he is a specialist (preferably board certified) in the field. Then show him the exams you were given by the VA as well as all your personal medical records on this issue. Ask him if he concurs with their exam. If he doesn't, get him to put it in writing and cite the different tests that he performed to support his conclusions. If he can cite any medical studies, that would make his statements stronger too. Thus you beat them at their own game. When you write it up, make sure you had the "COMPLETE" C&P exam done by a private doc and the VA doc's refused to perform the proper tests. Under the reasonable doubt rule, you have proven your case, and they failed to prove theirs. Get the doctor to explain the disease and the disease process, and the way it develops and what it can lead to, as well as describing the tests that prove or disprove its existence. Let the doctor describe a little of the misery involved. Then after you have agreed as to what needs to be done schedule the client for that examination. That raises you to a reasonable level of function as to the medical aspects. This way the doctor is explaining the disease to the adjudicator so the adjudicator will understand the disease and better informed and able to make a fair decision.

20.   Idiot Proofing Your Claim

List every time you went to the doctor, provide a copy of that medical record, highlighted the medical record and bunched them together in a group so the claims examiner does not have to hunt for the information. You need to idiot proof the claim! You need to give your claim to a third party and see if they can find holes in your arguments. Try and anticipated the weaknesses in the claim and find the law or regulation that turned the weakness into a strong point.

21.   Finalizing Your Claim

After you finished pulling your information together, you need to find an organization that will represent you before the Veterans Administration. If there is any supporting evidence you cannot find, either the veteran's representative can try and find it or the VA is required under the Veterans Claims Assistance Act to find the documentation for you. You need to point out what documentation they need to assist you and you need to provide them enough information necessary to find it (Who, What, When, Where and How Much).

Who can file?

At any point after you have completed military service, you may file an application for disability compensation. Here are the basic tests:

- you believe that military service has caused an injury or illness (called a "condition" by the VA) or
- you believe that a preexisting condition was aggravated by military service.

There are no time limits or restrictions except in a few very limited circumstances. As a general rule, you may seek disability compensation at any time for any condition that you reasonably believe was caused or aggravated by your service.

Can I file a claim myself? Do I need a lawyer?

The initial filing of a claim is simple. You may file the appropriate forms yourself or get help from an accredited Veterans Service Officer who will likely work for a Veterans Service Organization or a State Veterans Service Office. You are not allowed to pay anyone to represent you at this stage of the process.

How do I know whether it's worth filing a claim?

Let's assume you are going to represent yourself in this claim. Before you file, you'll need to understand the basic requirements.

1. **Eligible military service:** You must have done military service, and you must have a discharge that is other than dishonorable. If your discharge is other than honorable but not dishonorable, you may be qualified for only some types of benefits. Go here for information about challenging your discharge status.

2. **Current "condition":** You must have a current injury or illness (condition) that can be connected to your military service. This means that you should have a fairly clear diagnosis. It should be stated in a medical record prepared by a qualified health care provider (preferably a doctor). The more precisely defined the condition is in the record, the better.

3. **Evidence:** You must have evidence to support your claim. The best evidence is an event that is recorded in a Service Medical Record (SMR). This is a detailed description of the cause of the injury or illness leading to your condition, how it was treated, and any residual effects of the event. If the condition is related to a non-combat event, you will need documentation of:

4. **A clear service connection:** Your medical evidence must be clear enough to prove that your current condition is connected to the in-service event. This is called **"service connection"** or **"nexus."** If you can't prove the service connection, you will not receive benefits.

What else do I need to know?

I suggest that you consider another set of requirements before you file a claim. You should be **well organized** and prepared to deal with a lot **of paperwork**, including copying of files and searching for evidence. It helps if you:

- are familiar with searching for records on the Internet,
- know how to use a word processor,
- own or have access to a scanner and copier
- are confident that you have the patience to deal with details.

The VA process, even at its best, is slow, prone to error, and requires constant attention. You are much more likely to be successful if you can organize your information and keep good records of interactions with VA. If you believe that you meet these requirements, I encourage you to apply for your deserved benefits. If you have trouble with these kinds of tasks, you may want to seek help from a VSO or your state veterans affairs office.

NOTE: If it's not too late for you, plan ahead. The process can be much easier for military members who are still serving,. Once you file a VA claim, your Service Medical Record is sent to the VA by your branch of service. Thus, if a soldier visits medical for claimable injuries and builds a sound medical history of the injury while still in service, the process could simply involve filing a claim, going through a VA medical examination (if necessary), and waiting to hear back about your disability rating. Your military records become your VA evidence. Therefore, through good prior planning, veterans can avoid much of the headache involved in the claim process

Disability Compensation and Pension

I. Compensation Benefit Description

The VA compensation program provides you monthly benefits if you are disabled because of an injury or disease incurred in or aggravated during your military service and for certain conditions which may develop after your release from active duty. Benefits are authorized based upon the severity of your claimed disability(ies). If your service-connected disabilities are evaluated as 30 percent or more, you are entitled to additional allowances for your dependents.

Other Benefits/Payments May Affect Your VA Compensation

Military Retired Pay - By law, the payment of VA compensation benefits is affected by the receipt of military retired pay. If you receive military retirement, you may initiate a waiver of your retired pay to receive the full amount of VA compensation. Until the waiver takes effect, your compensation will be adjusted or withheld depending on the amount of military retired pay you are entitled to. The advantage of waiving military retired pay for VA compensation is that VA benefits are not taxable.

Disability Severance Pay - By law, payment of VA compensation and military disability severance pay for the same medical condition or disability is prohibited. VA compensation will be withheld on a monthly basis until the total amount of military severance pay has been recovered. Special Separation Benefit (SSB) - VA compensation will be withheld in full until the amount of the SSB has been recovered.

Voluntary Separation Incentive (VSI) - Your annual VSI payment will be reduced by an amount equal to the amount of VA compensation paid for the same period.

Selected Reserve and National Guard - By law, if you are an active member of the Selected Reserve or National Guard, your VA compensation will be withheld at the rate of one day of pay for each drill period served. Also, VA compensation is not payable while serving full-time on active duty.

II. Eligibility

You may be entitled to VA disability compensation for any medical condition or injury that was incurred in or aggravated by your military service if you were released from active military duty with an other than dishonorable discharge. There is no time limit to apply for VA disability compensation. However, you are encouraged to apply within one year of your release from active duty as entitlement is established retroactively to the date of separation if your claim is filed within this period. The effective date of eligibility for benefits will be based upon the date of your claim if you apply beyond the one-year period.

III. How to Apply - Burlington, Mass. Residents

(Note from Burlington Office of Veterans' Services: We generally suggest that VA Form 21-4138, Statement in Support of Claim, be sent in first. The VA always sends the veteran the 21-526 even if a completed one is

sent with the Statement of Claim causing great confusion to the veteran, so we suggest sending it after the VA has notified the veteran that they are working on their claim. The Burlington Office of Veterans' Services recommends that all veterans have a service organization represent them, i.e., Mass Office of Veterans' Services, V.F.W., D.A.V., V.V.A., etc.

Note: If the following pdf sites do not open, register here for the Acrobat Reader software PDF format program. http://www.adobe.com/products/acrobat/readstep.html)

Submit VA Form 21-4138 - Statement in Support of Claim

VA FORM 21-4138 - Statement in Support of Claim

Veteran completes Form 21-4138 by simply making a statement in connection with a claim for benefits and adds on that form that he/she would like to be evaluated by the VA. After the VA receives the Statement of Claim, they will forward to the veteran Form 21-526. (This form can be downloaded here and started.)

VA FORM 21-526 - Veterans Application for Compensation or Pension

Instructions and form to complete for Compensation or Pension. Read all the instructions.

VA FORM 21-22 Appointment of Veterans Service Organization as Claimant's Representative

This form gives a service organization permission to help the veteran or veteran's family member. Copies of all correspondence sent to the veteran will be sent to an organization's mailing address.

The following supporting evidence and/or documents should be submitted with your application:

Service Medical Records - Those applicants who have their service medical records are encouraged to submit them with their application to expedite processing. Otherwise, VA will contact the service department to obtain them.

Other Medical Records - Medical records to substantiate any and all treatment by private doctors and hospitals. **Dependency Documents** - Original or copies of birth and marriage certificates and copies of divorce/death record terminating all of your prior marriages and those of your spouse.

Military Discharge/DD Form 214 - (Copy 4 - Member Copy) Those applicants who have a copy of their DD-214 are encouraged to provide a copy with their claim to expedite processing. Otherwise, VA will attempt to obtain verification from the service department.

IV. Other Related Benefits

- Priority Inpatient and Outpatient Medical Care
- Prosthetics, Sensory and Rehabilitative Aids
- Clothing Allowance
- Automobile Grant
- Vocational Rehabilitation
- Disabled Veterans Life Insurance
- Preference for Employment in the Federal Government
- Job Finding Assistance
- Specially Adapted Housing Grant
- Burial Benefits
- Dependents Educational Assistance Program
- Medical Care for Dependents and Survivors (CHAMPVA) http://www.va.gov/hac/forbeneficiaries/champva/champva.asp
- Certain State and Local Benefits

DISABILITY PENSION

VA Pension Programs

This web site is intended to be an information resource for veterans, surviving spouses and children who might be eligible for VA's Pension Benefits. Pension benefits are meant as an assistance for eligible veterans, surviving spouses and children who demonstrate financial need.

VA manages two broad categories of Pension Benefits Programs:

1.) Veterans Pension and

2.) Spouse and Child Pension.

Click link for more information: http://www.vba.va.gov/bln/21/pension/index.htm

Source: VA.gov

10% - 20% (With or Without Dependents)

Percentage	Rate
10%	$127
20%	$251

30% - 60% Without Children

Dependent Status	30	40	50	60
Veteran Alone	$389	$560	$797	$1009
Veteran with Spouse Only	$435	$622	$874	$1102
Veteran with Spouse & One Parent	$472	$671	$936	$1176
Veteran with Spouse and Two Parents	$509	$720	$998	$1250
Veteran with One Parent	$426	$609	$859	$1083
Veteran with Two Parents	$463	$658	$921	$1157
Additional for A/A spouse (see footnote b)	$42	$56	$71	$84

70% - 100% Without Children

Dependent Status	70	80	90	100
Veteran Alone	$1,272	$1,478	$1,661	$2,769
Veteran with Spouse Only	$1,380	$1,602	$1,800	$2,924
Veteran with Spouse & One Parent	$1,466	$1,701	$1,911	$3,048
Veteran with Spouse and Two Parents	$1,552	$1,800	$2,022	$3,172
Veteran with One Parent	$1,358	$1,577	$1,772	$2,893
Veteran with Two Parents	$1,444	$1,676	$1,883	$3,017
Additional for A/A spouse (see footnote b)	$99	$112	$127	$141

30% - 60% With Children

Dependent Status	30%	40%	50%	60%
Veteran with Spouse & Child	$469	$667	$931	$1169
Veteran with Child Only	$420	$601	$849	$1071
Veteran with Spouse, One Parent and Child	$506	$716	$993	$1243
Veteran with Spouse, Two Parents and Child	$543	$765	$1055	$1,317
Veteran with One Parent and Child	$457	$650	$911	$1145
Veteran with Two Parents and Child	$494	$699	$973	$1219
Add for Each Additional Child Under Age 18	$23	$30	$38	$46
Each Additional Schoolchild Over Age 18 (see footnote a)	$74	$99	$124	$148
Additional for A/A spouse (see footnote b)	$42	$56	$71	$84

70% - 100% **With Children**

Dependent Status	70%	80%	90%	100%
Veteran with Spouse & Child	$1,459	$1,692	$1,902	$3,037
Veteran with Child Only	$1,344	$1,561	$1,754	$2,873
Veteran with Spouse, One Parent and Child	$1,545	$1,791	$2,013	$3,161
Veteran with Spouse, Two Parents and Child	$1,631	$1,890	$2,124	$3,285
Veteran with One Parent and Child	$1,430	$1,660	$1,865	$2,997
Veteran with Two Parents and Child	$1,516	$1,759	$1,976	$3,121
Add for Each Additional Child Under Age 18	$53	$61	$69	$77
Each Additional Schoolchild Over Age 18 (see footnote a)	$173	$198	$223	$248
Additional for A/A spouse (see footnote b)	$99	$112	$127	$141

FOOTNOTES:

- **A.** Rates for each school child are shown separately. They are not included with any other compensation rates. All other entries on this chart reflecting a rate for children show the rate payable for children under 18 or helpless. To find the amount payable to a 70% disabled veteran with a spouse and four children, one of whom is over 18 and attending school, take the 70% rate for a veteran with a spouse and 3 children, $ 1,565, and add the rate for one school child, $173. The total amount payable is $1,738.

- **B.** Where the veteran has a spouse who is determined to require Aid and Attendance (A/A), add the figure shown as "additional for A/A spouse" to the amount shown for the proper dependency code. For example, veteran has A/A spouse and 2 minor children and is 70% disabled. Add $99, additional for A/A spouse, to the rate for a 70% veteran with dependency code 12, $1,512. The total amount payable is $ 1,611.

These rates were provided by the Department of Veterans Affairs. The original copies can be found at: http://www.vba.va.gov/bln/21/Rates/comp01.htm.

VA Travel Reimbursement

Reimbursement for mileage or public transportation may be paid to the following:

1. Veterans with service-connected disabilities rated at 30% or more;
2. Veterans traveling for treatment of a service-connected condition;
3. Veterans receiving a VA pension;
4. Veterans traveling for scheduled compensation or pension examinations;
5. Veterans whose income does not exceed the maximum VA pension rate;

Mileage Reimbursement is at the rate of 41.5 cents per mile. These milieage subject to a deductible of $3 for a one way trip, $6 for a round trip, with a maximum of $18 per or the amount after six one-way trips (whichever occurs first) per calendar month. However, these deductibles can be waived if they cause a financial hardship to the veteran.

The deductible is also waived for veterans traveling for scheduled compensation or pension examinations

Disabled veterans can collect Social Security disability benefits and veterans disaiblity benefits at the same time, so disabled vets will usually find themselves dealing with the Social Security Administration at one point or another. Many vets may end up very surprised when they learn how different the two systems are. In this article, we'll discuss the principal aspects of the SSA system as well as the differences that exist between the two systems.

How Does Social Security Disability Work?

A person applies for disability benefits at a Social Security office or online, and receives an initial decision within three to four months. The claimant's file is assigned to a disability examiner, a specialist who will gather the claimant's medical records and, then, in consultation with a physician and/or a psychologist who is assigned to the examiner's unit, make an approval decision or denial decision. Unfortunately, the decision that is made is typically a denial. If the claim is approved, the claimant is considered 100% disabled, and will be paid either SSDI benefits based on their prior wages or SSI benefits based on the amount of income they have (only those with low income and low assets qualify for SSI).

If the claim is denied, the claimant may follow the appeal process and get a recondiseration review and then, after a vrey long wait, get a hearing with an administrative law judge. may take an extremely long time to have a hearing date set. Depending on which part of the country the claimant resides in, and how backlogged their local hearing office is, it may take a year or longer to have a hearing date set.

How Is the Social Security Disability System Different From the VA System?

Primarily, the SSA system is different from the VA system in that there are no percentages of disability. While the veterans disability system allows the VA to conclude that a vet is 10% or 40% or 100% disabled and then receive benefits based on that determination, in the Social Security system, it is all or nothing.

Without a doubt, the SSA system is fairly draconian. In fact, the definition of disablity used by the Social Security system stipulates that not only must your condition keep you out of work , but your disability must also last or be expected to last for at least one year or to result in death.

There are other aspects of Social Security disability that veterans should probably know about. First of all, if your primary source of treatment is a VA medical center, don't assume that the disability examiner who is assigned to your case will be successful in obtaining your VA medical records. The VA is notorious in some areas for not supplying needed medical records to the Social Security Administration (SSA). For this reason, it's never a bad idea for vets to personally obtain their medical records themselves so they may turn these records in to the SSA when they apply for disability or file an appeal. One word of caution, though: never submit anything to Social Security without making a copy first, since the SSA is fairly notorious for loosing things that have been sent to them.

What About the Role of Attorneys?

In the Social Security system, an attorney works off a contingency-fee basis from the moment they represent a claimant. In other words, if they win the case, they get paid up to 25% of whatever backpay that SSA decides it owes the claimant. The corollary of this, of course, is that the attorney receives nothing if the case is not won.

Is an attorney always needed in a Social Security disability case? No, and, in fact, there are many outstanding disability representatives who are not attorneys and are referred to as "non-attorney representatives" (some of these non-attorney reps are former Social Security employees who put their experience to use representing disabled individuals).

The rule of thumb for getting an attorney (or non-attorney rep) is usually this. If you get denied on your initial claim, you should probably get an attorney, because you can appeal until you get a hearing in front of a judge, and it will help to have an experienced representative at your side during the hearing.

by: Beth Laurence, J.D.

Go to Title 38 Part 4, to review all of the rules concerning your claim, this is the regulation they will use to determine your case. You must have some of the key words in your medical records in order to be awarded a claim.

http://ecfr.gpoaccess.gov/cgi/t/text/text-idx?c=ecfr&sid=0f067325c23fe3873bdc40d2c54423d1&tpl=/ecfrbrowse/Title38/38cfr4_main_02.tpl

Example:

The Foot

	Rating
5276 Flatfoot, acquired:	
Pronounced; marked pronation, extreme tenderness of plantar surfaces of the feet, marked inward displacement and severe spasm of the tendo achillis on manipulation, not improved by orthopedic shoes or appliances	
Bilateral	50
Unilateral	30
Severe; objective evidence of marked deformity (pronation, abduction, etc.), pain on manipulation and use accentuated, indication of swelling on use, characteristic callosities:	
Bilateral	30
Unilateral	20
Moderate; weight-bearing line over or medial to great toe, inward bowing of the tendo achillis, pain on manipulation and use of the feet, bilateral or unilateral	10
Mild; symptoms relieved by built-up shoe or arch support	0
5277 Weak foot, bilateral:	
A symptomatic condition secondary to many constitutional conditions, characterized by atrophy of the musculature, disturbed circulation, and weakness:	
Rate the underlying condition, minimum rating	10
5278 Claw foot (pes cavus), acquired:	
Marked contraction of plantar fascia with dropped forefoot, all toes hammer toes, very painful callosities, marked varus deformity:	
Bilateral	50

Unilateral	30
All toes tending to dorsiflexion, limitation of dorsiflexion at ankle to right angle, shortened plantar fascia, and marked tenderness under metatarsal heads:	
Bilateral	30
Unilateral	20
Great toe dorsiflexed, some limitation of dorsiflexion at ankle, definite tenderness under metatarsal heads:	
Bilateral	10
Unilateral	10
Slight	0
5279 Metatarsalgia, anterior (Morton's disease), unilateral, or bilateral	10
5280 Hallux valgus, unilateral:	
Operated with resection of metatarsal head	10
Severe, if equivalent to amputation of great toe	10
5281 Hallux rigidus, unilateral, severe:	
Rate as hallux valgus, severe.	
Note: Not to be combined with claw foot ratings.	
5282 Hammer toe:	
All toes, unilateral without claw foot	10
Single toes	0
5283 Tarsal, or metatarsal bones, malunion of, or nonunion of:	
Severe	30
Moderately severe	20
Moderate	10
Note: With actual loss of use of the foot, rate 40 percent.	
5284 Foot injuries, other:	
Severe	30
Moderately severe	20
Moderate	10
Note: With actual loss of use of the foot, rate 40 percent.	

Go to the U.S. Department of Veterans Affairs website and download Form 21-526 (see references). This form can be filled out online and printed or can be printed and filled in at that time.

Gather your active duty information needed to complete Section A of the form. Have unit information, including addresses and dates served, readily available to insert into the application. Attach an original Form DD-214 or other separation papers as proof of service for this section of the application.

List any disabilities that you are claiming for compensation through the VA in Section B. Include information about the type of disability or illness, when it occurred, treatment being received and information on exposures or events that may have contributed to the disability. Attach copies of all service medical records, current medical records and any information that substantiates your claim that the disability is a result of military service.

Complete spousal information including date of birth and social security number. List any information regarding previous marriages. List all information for children currently living with you including social security numbers and dates of birth. Also list the same information for children not currently living with you including any child support payments that are paid. Attach copies of marriage certificates, divorce decrees, birth certificates and adoption papers for every person previously listed.

Sign and date the application. Make a copy of the application for your records. Mail the application to the closest VA office (see references).

What VA Does after It Receives Your Claim

After VA receives your *Application for Compensation*, it sends you a letter. The letter explains what VA needs in order to help grant your claim. It states how VA assists in getting records to support your claim. The letter may include forms for you to complete, such as medical releases. They help VA obtain pertinent medical records from your doctor or hospital. You should try to complete and return all forms VA sends within a month. Your claim can often be processed more quickly if you send a copy of your own medical records.

What Records VA Obtains to Support Your Claim

VA then attempts to get all the records relevant to your claimed medical conditions from the military, private hospitals or doctors, or any other place you tell us. The person who decides your claim (called a Rating Veterans Service Representative) may order a medical examination. This examination is free of charge. It is extremely important that you report for your examination at the scheduled time to avoid delaying your claim.

What to Expect during the Medical Examination

You should expect the examiner performing your medical examination to evaluate the condition(s) listed on your claim for benefits. Depending on the number and type of disabilities claimed, the length of the examination will vary. Psychiatric examination or that for multiple disabilities requires more time to evaluate. The examiner may ask more questions about your disability's history, review pertinent medical records, or order additional testing or examinations, if necessary. *The examination will not include any form of treatment for disabilities or acute illnesses.* Unless additional information, tests, or evaluations are needed, the completed evaluation will be documented and forwarded to the VA Regional Office for processing.

What VA Does after Obtaining Your Records After the Rating Veterans Service Representative has attempted to secure all the records (or evidence) required by law (including the report of any examinations), he/she reviews your file and makes a decision on the claim according to the law and the particular facts in your case. In the rating decision, the Rating Veterans Service Representative lists the evidence, the decision, and the reasons for it. VA then sends the decision with a cover letter. If benefits are granted, the letter provides the monthly payment amount and the effective date. Payments usually begin soon after you receive the letter of your award. However, if benefits are not granted and you think the decision was in error, or if you think the percentage evaluation or effective date is wrong, you may appeal by requesting a reconsideration which is the best, or request and appeal by writing a formal letter of disagreement with new and material evidence or a reason you believe you should be granted a percentage.

GETTING STARTED
Frequently Asked Questions
About Appeals

What is an appeal?

An appeal is a request for the Board of Veterans' Appeals to review a local VA office decision on your claim.

Why would I appeal?

You appeal because you are not satisfied with the decision by the local VA office.

The two most common reasons people appeal are:

- The VA denied you benefits for a disability you believe began in service; or
- You believe that your disability is more severe than the VA rated it.

You can appeal for any reason.

What is the Board of Veterans' Appeals?

The Board of Veterans' Appeals (also known as the Board or BVA) is a part of the Department of Veterans Affairs. It is located in Washington, D.C. Members of the Board review appeals for VA benefits and make decisions on those appeals.

Statement of the Case (SOC)

After the local VA office gets your NOD it will create a "Statement of the Case" (SOC).

VA gets your NOD

What is a Statement of the Case?

The SOC is a detailed explanation of the evidence, laws, and regulations used by the local VA office in deciding your claim.

VA prepares SOC

Who sends the SOC?

The SOC will be mailed to you along with a VA Form 9, Substantive Appeal Form by your local VA office.

SOC is mailed to you

Additional Information
& Internet Resources

National Archives and Records Administration
Code of Federal Regulations
www.access.gpo.gov/nara/cfr
Published federal regulations, including 38 C.F.R., used by VA

The Office of the Law Revision Counsel
U.S. House of Representatives
uscode.house.gov/usc.htm
Search and print the United States Code, including 38 U.S.C.,
used by VA

Information about Veterans' Benefits
1-800-827-1000

Information about your appeal at the Board
1-202-565-5436

DEFINITIONS

In order to make our communications as clear as possible, we'd like to define some of our terms:

Compensation: The benefit paid to veterans whose disabilities arose from service. The disabilities themselves are often referred to as Service Connected or "S/C".

Pension: The benefit paid to veterans whose disabilities are not related to service and who have a financial hardship. The disabilities themselves are often referred to as Non-Service Connected or "NSC".

Rating Schedule: The guide we use to determine which disabilities we can pay for and the percent to which they are disabling.

Claim Number: How we monitor and identify your claim. Any letters you receive from this office should have the claim number in the upper right hand corner. The letters "C", "XC", "CSS" or "XSS" will precede your claim number. It is very important that you have this number available whenever you contact this office.

Appeals of Decisions

An appeal of a local decision involves many steps, some optional and some necessary, and strict time limits. In order, the steps are:

Notice of Disagreement (NOD)
Statement of the Case (SOC)
Formal Appeal (VA Form 9 or equivalent)
Hearings (Optional)
Board of Veterans' Appeals (BVA)
United States Court of Appeals for Veterans' Claims (CAVC)
The case may also involve remands at the BVA and/or COVA levels. Someone may have several appeals at once, and several issues may be included in the same appeal. Usually, all issues on one VA decision will be included in the same appeal.

Notice of Disagreement (NOD)

A Notice of Disagreement is the first step in an appeal. It simply involves a written statement that you disagree with a decision that has been made. Certain things should be kept in mind when submitting a NOD:

Be specific about what you are disagreeing with. If a decision was made on 7 issues, specify the ones you are referring to- don't simply say you disagree with the decision.

Make sure that a decision has been made. For most decisions when benefits are reduced or terminated, we are required to propose it first; this is called a pre-determination notice. A NOD can only be accepted if a final decision has been made, not if a proposal has been made. If you don't receive paperwork describing the appeals process (a VA Form 4107), check your letter to see if it is a proposal.

Check the time limit. A NOD must be filed within one year of the date of the letter informing you of the decision. If you were notified of a decision in 1994, it is too late to file a NOD. Your option at that point is to file another claim, or request to reopen a claim, for the same condition as before.

Statement of the Case

A Statement of the Case is a summary of the evidence considered, actions taken, and decisions made, plus the laws governing the decision. A SOC must be done when a Notice of Disagreement is filed or when new evidence is received. Once the first SOC is done on an appeal, any ones done after that is Supplemental Statements of the Case (SSOC). An appeal may have several SSOC's.

Formal Appeal (VA Form 9 or equivalent)

An appeal must be formal before it can continue to higher levels. The standard form for formalizing (sometimes called perfecting) an appeal is the VA Form 9. This form must be received no later than one of these two dates:

one year from the date of the letter notifying you of the decision
60 days after the date of the Statement of the Case
Hearings (Optional)

Hearings are a chance for claimants to present evidence in person; they are totally optional. They are held at the regional office by a Hearing Officer (HO). If you have a hearing, the HO will review the evidence in conjunction with the testimony and make a decision on your case. If the issue is not resolved in your favor, the appeal will continue.

Board of Veterans' Appeals (BVA)

The Board of Veterans Appeals, located in Washington DC, is the highest appellate body in VA. Although most decision is done in Washington, BVA does have travel boards that come to local offices. Travel boards have been limited the past couple of years, and Manchester would not expect more than one week of travel board hearings in a year. Due to a number of reasons, the pending workload at BVA has dramatically increased in the past few years. It is not unusual for an appeal to take 2 years or more from the initial NOD to the final BVA decision.

BVA looks at all of the evidence regarding the issue under appeal. If BVA decides that more information is needed to make a decision, it will issue a remand to the local office. BVA will not reconsider the case until its instructions in the remand are done. If the evidence is sufficient, BVA will issue a decision. This decision is the final VA one on the issue, and the appeal will have ended. However, a BVA decision can be reviewed by the Court of Veterans Appeals if an appeal to the court is filed within 120 days of the BVA decision.

United States Court of Appeals for Veterans' Claims (CAVC)

The United States Court of Appeals for Veterans' Claims (CAVC), located in Washington DC, was created in 1988 to review matters of law about VA benefits and decisions. CAVC is not part of VA; it is an appellate court in the US judicial system. CAVC will only consider decisions made by the Board of Veterans Appeals after 1988. As in most courts, one must have either an attorney or personal knowledge of legal proceedings in order to file the correct legal paperwork and conduct the appeal. CAVC decisions usually concern the procedural, legal issues involved in the "letter of the law". The deadline for filing an appeal to COVA is 120 days after the BVA decision (using the date of the letter to you informing you of the decision).

Communicating with the Veterans Service Center

COMMUNICATION IS NOT ONLY WHAT WE SAY, IT'S WHAT YOU THINK WE SAID.

If you get a letter from the VA that is confusing, please let us know. We are truly interested in improving our communication. When doing so, provide the date of the letter in question.

In all correspondence to the VA please provide:

The VA claim number
Veteran's social security number
Veteran's complete name

Please be sure to keep them informed of address changes.

National Personnel Records Center
The National Personnel Records Center (NPRC), located in St. Louis, is the main center for a military person's records. NPRC has millions of records. Depending on the branch and years of service, we will make a request for records to NPRC. If medical records are available at NPRC, the originals will be sent to us. No copies are left at NPRC. Any individual can request their records from NPRC using a standard form (SF 180), which we can provide to you upon request. However, to reduce the substantial backlog at NPRC, duplicate requests from VA, individuals, and/or service organizations should not be made at the same time. If you receive notification from us those records could not be located, you may find it more efficient to deal with NPRC directly

Fire-related case
In July 1973, and a fire broke out at NPRC. The majority of records for Army and Air Force veterans discharged before 1963 were destroyed. There are no alternate sources for personnel or other non-medical records. In the late 1980's, there were Surgeon General studies discovered that listed names of patients treated in Army hospitals during World War II and the Korean War. These records, usually containing only one line of information, can be requested if you were treated in an Army hospital during one of the wars. Unfortunately, there remain no alternate sources for the other burned records.

Reservists

If you are a reservist, you may want to request that your unit forward a copy of your medical records to this office. If you are filing a claim for a disability that occurred while you were on reserve duty, we also need a copy of the paperwork showing your duty status on the day you were injured. We frequently experience significant delays in receiving records from reserve units.

PTSD

PTSD cases often take several months to process. In order to establish a finding of PTSD, as opposed to other mental conditions, the event causing the stress disorder (the stressor) must be identified. Sometimes the stressor is apparent on the discharge document (for example, a Purple Heart). Often, we must request personnel and other records from the National Personnel Records Center. However, while personnel records will show units, job classifications, etc., they do not show events that happened. For those records, we must make an additional request to another records center for information they may have on particular events. This search is why we need as specific information as possible on the stressor form that we send (names, dates, units, etc.). The current backlog at this records center is several months. This time, added what it takes to get records from NPRC, is why PTSD cases take longer to process.

DISCLAIMER

I'm not a lawyer. I don't play lawyer. I don't pretend to have anywhere close to a legal mindset. This isn't legal advice. I refer a lot of veterans to lawyers because I have limits to my knowledge. I'm offering this advice to you based on my personal experiences as well as what I've learned from others over the years. The process of filing a claim for disability compensation at the VA is not supposed to be a legal process, it's an administrative process.

References used in these publications:

http://www.vba.va.gov/bln/21/Topics/claims.htm

http://vawatchdog.org/how%20to%20file%20a%20claim.htm

http://www.vetshome.com/how_to_file_a_va_claim.htm

http://www.va.gov

www.dav.org

The following are excerpts from cases that have been adjudicated over the years, and sections of pertinent code. These lists are by no means complete, but look through it and see if there is anything that applies to your situation. You can type these case laws and place them on your statement in support of claims to ensure the VSO knows that you are aware of your right to have lay statements. And get statements from everyone, your dad, friend, wife, girlfriend, boyfriend anyone that has any knowledge of your condition. Have them state how your condition has gotten worse and how your social life has been affected. Use VA form 21-4138 (Statement in Support of Claim). You can also do the claim online at Ebenefits:
https://www.ebenefits.va.gov/ebenefits-portal/ebenefits.portal

38 U.S.C.A. § 5107 (West 2002); 38 C.F.R. § 3.102 (2009)

When there is an approximate balance of evidence regarding the merits of an issue material to the determination of the matter, the benefit of the doubt in resolving each such issue shall be given to the claimant.

Gilbert v. Derwinski, 1 Vet. App. 49, 53 (1990)

The United States Court of Appeals for Veterans Claims (the Court) stated that "a veteran need only demonstrate that there is an 'approximate balance of positive and negative evidence' in order to prevail."

38 U.S.C.A. § 5103A (West 2002); 38 C.F.R. § 3.159 (2009)

In general, the VCAA provides that VA shall make reasonable efforts to assist a claimant in obtaining evidence necessary to substantiate claims for VA benefits, unless no reasonable possibility exists that such assistance would aid in substantiating the claims. The law provides that the assistance provided by VA shall include providing a medical examination or obtaining a medical opinion when such an examination or opinion is necessary to make a decision on the claims. An examination is deemed "necessary" if the record does not contain sufficient medical evidence for VA to make a decision on the claims.

Coburn v. Nicholson, 19 Vet. App. 427 (2006).

A medical opinion cannot be disregarded solely on the rationale that the medical opinion is based on a history provided by the veteran.

Jandreau v. Nicholson, 492 F.3d 1372, 1377 (Fed. Cir. 2007)

Depending on the evidence and contentions of record in a particular case, lay evidence can be competent and sufficient to establish a diagnosis of a condition.

38 C.F.R. § 3.159(a)(2); see also Layno v. Brown, 6 Vet. App. 471 (1994).

Lay persons are competent to provide evidence regarding things they have personally observed, including symptoms that are capable of lay observation and when those symptoms occurred.

Buchanan v. Nicholson, 451 F.3d 1331, 1137 (Fed. Cir. 2006)

The Board cannot determine that lay evidence lacks credibility merely because it is unaccompanied by contemporaneous medical evidence.

Clemons v. Shinseki, 23 Vet. App. 1 (2009)

The Board notes that the Veteran's claim constituted a claim for service connection for an acquired sychiatric disability, however diagnosed. As such, the claim must be considered a claim for service connection for any and all psychiatric disabilities clinically indicated.

The veteran is competent as a lay person to report that on which he has personal knowledge. See Layno v. Brown, 6 Vet. App. 465, 470 (1994).

DISCLAIMER

I'm not a lawyer. I don't play lawyer. I don't pretend to have anywhere close to a legal mindset. This isn't legal advice. I refer a lot of veterans to lawyers because I have limits to my knowledge. I'm offering this advice to you based on my personal experiences as well as what I've learned from others over the years. The process of filing a claim for disability compensation at the VA is not supposed to be a legal process, it's an administrative process.

"There are No Limitations To The Mind Except Those We Acknowledge"

www.ingramcontent.com/pod-product-compliance
Lightning Source LLC
Chambersburg PA
CBHW081540280526
45788CB00010B/3307